OCT 2 3 2015

D0097661

august 24   september 22

virgo

WS
WHITE STAR PUBLISHERS

contents

Text by
Patrizia Troni

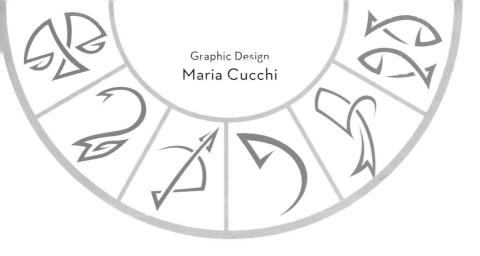

Graphic Design
Maria Cucchi

Character and Temperament

The Virgo character has two fundamental characteristics; some times, they are of equal importance and, at other time, one prevails over the other. Virgo is distinguished by great mental and intellectual activity, but is also extremely practical and concrete. Sometimes the cerebral part dominates, thus generating thought that never ceases, that is always active, seemingly endless. This may well become an overflowing torrent, which is accompanied by an elevated critical and self-critical consciousness. On the one hand, this continuous flow of thought makes Virgo one of the most subtle, refined and intelligent of the Zodiac signs, while, on the other hand, it becomes almost a torment, endless reflection that disregards real needs and sentiments.

While it is true that it is fundamental for Virgo to understand matters, even down to the minutest detail, it is also true that the pragmatic and realistic side of their personality ends up getting the upper hand, creating an urgency to do, to make and to work. The intellectual and practical sides can be united in the deepest essence of their character, which is the need to feel secure and tranquil when faced with the precarious nature and the ups and downs of existence.

3 0053
01081
6257

They are intelligent and concrete because they are attentive, prudent, scrupulous and wise. They need to keep everything under control because they do not want to be overwhelmed by anxiety and uncertainty. They want things to be clear, well-defined and they detest chaos and confusion. As Descartes would have said, for them, the truth must be clear and distinct, without improvisation, without unexpected events or changes that catch them by surprise.

This is the reason why order and precision are so crucial for Virgo. Life is much better if everything is in place and follows an order that will keep them from feeling immersed in a blurred, suspended state in moments of difficulty. They dislike risks and ventures and do not enjoy the prospect of a nebulous, ill-defined future. And, this need on their part is translated into conscientious activity, a connection with, and great attention paid to, everything around them. Therefore, in whatever they do they are reliable, devoted, engaged in a reality that consists, above all, of humble, methodical and regular action.

True, at times all this may be expressed in a manner that is somewhat affected and by no means instinctive.

Furthermore, their need to keep everything under control sometimes hinders relaxed and pleasant spontaneity. Yet their inclination for sacrifice and their serious, humble nature are precious instruments that allow them to cope with the, not always marvelous, surprises that existence springs on us. They are far-sighted, which is a truly precious quality.

One weakness in the Virgo character, which, from certain standpoints, might be considered a virtue as well, is their perfectionism, which makes them always dissatisfied with the results they achieve. This, almost compulsive, need to perform all of life's tasks and duties magnificently and scrupulously, the quality of which is very much appreciated by others, often ends up conditioning them too much and preventing them from savoring the fruits (including the psychological, emotional and sensual ones) of their impressive undertaking. Yet this is also one of the reasons why they have a conservative side that resists change: they cannot abide abandoning or neglecting, what they have constructed with such labor, in favor of something unknown and vague that may lead them god knows where.

Love and Passion

8 Virgo

In matters of love, Virgo also tends to search for a relationship that is not only a dream, poetry, fantasy, delicate kisses and sweet utterances. Rather, they prefer a bond that is somewhat realistic, concrete, and above all constant: they are practical and constructive even where strong romantic feeling is concerned. The couple that results, and true love, must never be something that confuses them or makes them uncertain because of irregular, destabilizing events. Love is a fundamental aspect of life, but it must be part of a broad context, acting as a stabilizing force and source of positive energy. Unlike other Zodiac signs, the Virgo personality is not ruled only by passion, explosive desire or an infinite need for affection. All of these aspects are important, to be sure, but they are not the only ones, and certainly not the only decisive ones. Besides these, love must also comprise awareness, realism, daily tranquility, a sense of reciprocal peace, the capacity to listen to one's partner, and a relationship marked by constancy. Love, sexual desire and romantic feelings must be compatible parts of a harmonious lifestyle in which everything has its place.

This does not mean that sensual pleasure and, openly manifested,

warm feelings interest them less. Naturally, they are fundamental, and by no means does Virgo look down on them; but they must not and cannot prevail over reason and the overall 'roadmap'.

Most Virgos are sexually and erotically uninhibited. In general, they are not repressed or uptight when it comes to sensual pleasure. Even a bit of imagination and 'nonconformist' variation is quite acceptable, especially if proposed by their partner, since they are not known for having an offbeat imagination. They are also tender, they like gentle sentiments and signs of affection, even though they must not be exaggerated and mechanical, because this nauseates them. They like to be cuddled rather than cuddle their partner, and it is precisely their occasional incapacity to openly manifest the tenderness they feel for the other person that might cause problems. They might even be accused of having a cold character, but this is not so. Although they are not capable of being mawkish and soppy, or of feigning feeling, this does not mean that their intimate self does not listen to their heart.

At the beginning of a relationship, they are one of the most faithful and constant signs, on a spiritual level, one of those most ready to listen to their partner. They are a solid point of reference, a pillar, for those they love. They listen to outpourings and give advice, but they often even solve practical problems and pull their partner's chestnuts out of the fire.

The male Virgo becomes tranquil and methodical, and perhaps a bit monotonous, in his tendency to plan and schedule his time rigorously, while the female Virgo, although she has a personality that makes her presence felt, willingly plays the role of a devoted geisha who follows her partner. She may even criticize him but never really challenges him, and her behavior is certainly not abusive of his trust, aggressive or destabilizing.

When all is said and done, in romantic matters Virgo wants peace and tranquility, they adore faithfulness and security. Their partner must reassure them that he/she will always stand by them, and it is precisely their infinite need for affection that makes them a bit servile, too traditional, and even somewhat submissive.

But, behind their concrete, composed, controlled, scarcely expansive and seemingly detached personality lies a spirit whose emotions are rich in nuances of affection and strong feeling that their partner – slowly, day by day – will learn to recognize and to accept as his/her own.

How to Hook a Virgo and How to Let Them Go

Virgos are supposedly cold, controlled, light years away from impulsive acts. Yet under the embers of this composure, there burns the typical Virgo heart, which wants nothing less than to be sparked by the fire of passion. For those born under Virgo, it is difficult to take the initiative or launch themselves headlong into a relationship. They prefer a long courtship in order to assess the validity and significance of the couple's feelings. They find it difficult to let go and give their emotions free rein; but when their heart finally surrenders, it overflows with tenderness.

In order to hook a Virgo male you must bear in mind that, often, he thinks only about his work and that surprise changes and moves will turn him to stone. To seduce him you must show him you are very solid, serious and reliable, and your attire must be classic and soberly elegant, not provocative and sensual. You must penetrate his heart very slowly, and gently, and behave like a geisha with him, sharing his hobbies and his little fads.

On your first date with a female Virgo, you must be a perfect gentleman, wear well-polished shoes, perfectly ironed shirt and jacket, and have your car washed. She is too well mannered a woman to make comments about a person's shortcomings, but she is also too critical and intelligent not to notice them. She will reject a disorderly, unkempt man immediately. In order to win her heart the man must be attentive and thoughtful, as well as determined if he wants to break down her resistance.

In order to break off a relationship with a Virgo you must tell them exactly when, how and why you have come to this decision. You must provide an 'analytical' explanation, complete with details regarding the dates, moments and situations during which your love story began to fall apart. Once a Virgo bows to the facts, he/she will not bear a grudge.

Compatibility with Other Signs

At first Virgo likes the overwhelming spontaneity of the Fire signs (Aries, Leo, and Sagittarius), but then their excessive irrationality and impulsiveness begin to irritate those Virgo nerves. There is no lack of tenderness in a couple, especially with a Leo partner, while, in theory at least, a relationship with an Aries or a Sagittarius risks becoming a roller coaster experience. With Taurus, Virgo makes an ideal couple, active and tops in their profession, solid as regards affection and erotically exhilarating. Virgo gets along rather well with Gemini, who, like Virgo, is also under the influence of Mercury. This means that both are cerebral, with thought processes that do not always dovetail with one another. Gemini is superficial while Virgo is precise. The danger of misunderstandings and cold feelings looms over this relationship. Scorpio is another cerebral sign, but it goes well with the Virgo gift for synthesis: it makes for a wonderful couple in work, while at home Scorpios tend to rule the roost and take advantage of the Virgo patience and, consequently, must be curbed every so often. Virgo is very fond of Libra and the feeling is mutual. Theoretically, it makes for a winning team in the work field, but domestic life as a couple is a bit jaded. With Cancer, on the other hand, Virgo enjoys magical moments and overwhelming abandon. For a sign like Virgo, that sometimes finds it difficult to express feelings, Cancer sensitivity is a soothing balm. The Cancer tenderness melts the Virgo heart, it envelops them like a soft cocoon, and although they might not always understand their inconstancy and irrationality, Virgo will forgive them without hesitation. Virgo is in splendid material, practical and mental harmony with Capricorn and Aquarius. Naturally, Virgo makes a perfect couple with another Virgo, but there may be a risk of the relationship becoming a bit boring. With Pisces, Virgo has fiery emotions, fatal attractions, perhaps because they are diametrically opposed in both character and the way they love. But then, as we know, opposites attract.

Virgo Profession and Career

Work is something sacred for Virgo. It is the pillar of existence. If everybody were born under Virgo, the human race would consist of people who, from birth, learn to be industrious, constructive and transformative, above all with their hands. Work may not be top of the rankings for Virgo, but it does play a central role in their lives. Virgo is associated with work as an employee, partly because they do not like the risks and precarious nature of entrepreneurial activity; they were not born for impossible gambles and do not like to embark on something without precise planning beforehand and above all without being certain of the result. This is the reason that, often, Virgo prefers a modest but secure salary over earnings that may be great but entail a high probability of uncertainty and risk. They are not ambitious and have no yearning for narcissistic power that glories in itself and considers the attainment of an important position something that allows them to stand out in public and show the whole world how brilliant they are. On the contrary, their approach to work is marked by great humility, precision and rigor, and their reliability makes them a mainstay for the entire company or team.

Their superiors can rely on them, they know that they always give more than they ask for, that they are faithful and carry out their work in a spirit of absolute self-denial. This is complemented by the virtue (or defect) of perfectionism that is always attentive to details, with a concept of order that is yet another tool for achieving clear results. While there may be some exceptions – due to particular positions on their personal birth charts – their professional image is rarely criticized or disputed. Again, Virgo also has a certain sense of hierarchy, because just as they respect their duties and are reliable as much as, and perhaps even more than, their superiors, so when, with time, their career rewards them with positions of authority and responsibility, they expect their colleagues to work and produce like a perfect mechanism – formally impeccable and respectful of schedules and the goals to be attained.

Another of the Virgo virtues/shortcomings is their humility, their reserve, taking a step backward rather than forward. They are not used to elbowing their way in order to emerge. They accept praise and re-

✿ ✿ ✿ ✿ ✿ ✿ ✿

wards only when they know that they have really deserved them and agree to fill important positions only when they are certain that they can perform the duties well.

On a physical level, Virgo make an excellent worker, indefatigable and full of stamina. Their remarkable intelligence leads to their being assigned organizational tasks, but let us not forget that Virgo is associated with the symbolism of 'manual dexterity' and that a great many artisans are Virgos, especially those who produce small objects and highly precise mechanisms. In general, Virgo also has a good relationship with technology, becoming electronic engineers, micro-surgeons, experts in nanotechnology, as well as goldsmiths, blacksmiths, watchmakers, and employees in firms that produce high-precision mechanisms.

Other professions linked to Virgo are chemistry and pharmacology, and many general practitioners were born under Virgo. Symbolically, Virgo is connected to both white-collar workers, in the service industries, and to the working class. The Virgo gifts of precision and manual dexterity also produce excellent gardeners and botanists.

How Virgo Thinks and Reasons

Virgo has one of the most linear, logical and reliable intellects in the Zodiac. Virgo is not interested in being spectacular in their thought process; they do not look for the impossible solution or the amazing one that leaves everyone open-mouthed. Their intelligence is mostly pragmatic and rapid, and is applied with acumen to improve life. This intelligence, which usually has a rational, scientific, technological and technical approach, works like a perfect mechanism that never misfires.

With Virgo, their best quality is the attention they pay to detail. They are never superficial, nor do they express themselves with improvised ideas, say the first thing that comes to mind or heed senseless fantasies. They are humble, constant and methodical, proceeding step by step. They overlook or skip nothing when it comes to solving the equations of life. If there is a defect in their intelligence, it is that they are too intelligent. This means that their mind never stops working, there is always something to understand, to grasp, so that, at times, thinking for them becomes almost torture because their rational nature thrusts the emotional and sensitive part of their mind into a corner.

Their rationality is always impeccable and reliable; they never rely on inventions or chimeras: they evaluate actions very carefully before performing them, analyzing all the factors from every perspective. Their ability in abstracting and defining concepts is absolute yet is always firmly connected to practice. This is because, for them, thought must always be utilitarian. They must tend to improve whatever they are involved in. If a castle in the air arrives they must immediately build its foundations, otherwise they abandon this pipe dream and pass on to more concrete thoughts. Being attentive, rational and a good listener are among their most remarkable and spontaneous strong points: they are able to understand whomever they are talking to and know how to analyze the other person thanks to that capacity for thinking about others, which is certainly not a common gift.

Let us not forget that many philosophers were born under Virgo, beginning with the great German philosopher Hegel, who stated, in perfect Virgo style, that everything that is real is rational and that all truth is based on a clear definition of concepts.

Another quality of Virgo intelligence is its pragmatic-utilitarian approach; that is to say, they immediately know how to apply their keen mind to equally precise manual skills. Thus, their practical intelligence is never an end in itself but is, naturally, transformed into concrete acts. Their profound, refined and meticulous reasoning process might sometimes seem a bit cold or too finicky, given the great attention paid to details and the fact that they perhaps attach more importance to these latter than to the overview. But, in the long run, this intelligence is appreciated in all spheres because it does not aim at imposing its will or opinion on others, is never coarse and does not gloat about its conclusions, but is always vivacious, brilliant and attentive. Unlike other thinking modes, based on forms and appearance, and when they reason, they get right down to brass tacks. True, they may be a bit dry, detached, and essential and sometimes lacking in emotional empathy – or at least this is what some may accuse them of – but they never mistake a fleeting sensation (not to speak of fantasy or daydreams) for the truth.

Sociability, Communication

and Friendship

Virgo certainly could not be considered one of the most sociable of people, those who hop from one party to another and change company and friends at a breathtaking pace. No, they were not born for superficial, noisy jamborees in which one has no time to really get to know other people and everything is based on a frenetic rhythm good only for superficial contact. For Virgo, such get-togethers only end up disappointing. As regards sociability and communication, Virgo is decidedly selective and is fond of only a few people and certainly does not have thousands of people whom they consider as their friends. This selectivity stems from the fact that they do not trust immediate and spontaneous emotions. That mind of their, which is always at work and wants to keep everything under control, at times ends up being hypercritical and a bit too mistrustful. When they first meet someone, they seem to take a backward step, confining themselves to observing and studying the other person. What is crucial for them is to have enough time to transform acquaintanceship into true friendship. When time has cemented a relationship, deep and intimate friendship then serenely develops into a part of their life, until it becomes almost one of the many habits that are really the most reassuring things in life.

Virgo is never rowdy or rash, too outspoken or immediate with others. they do not like to overwhelm them with unbridled and fiery talk; they are always respectful of roles and contexts, and this, knowing how to behave, is yet another expression of their intelligence. Now this does not mean that they are closed or that they flee from cordial company. On the contrary, they appreciate company quite a lot, especially when others open up to them, reveal their feelings and trust them and their extraordinary gift of analysis. They are truly a precious friend, both when others need advice, be it only of a practical nature, and when they need to vent their feelings, or tell a secret. They take in and contain others' surges of emotion. Others confide in them because they know how to be trustful and they never speak indiscreetly or demean themselves with gossip. In short, they are appreciated as true, loyal friends.

Some might consider the fact that they continue to be thoughtful, measured and not too expansive in company and even with friends, to be a drawback. And, at times, their tendency to dot the i's and cross the t's too much, or to be critical and rigorous, might disturb those who prefer the effortlessness of a superficial approach. When they exaggerate in being finicky, they risk becoming boring, because, for others, they are difficult to follow in all the details of a matter. Whereas, it is those details that stimulate and excite you. When they must describe or explain a question, they scrutinize and even dissect it, while others, used to going directly to the heart of the matter, might begin to yawn if Virgo starts counting the trees to make sure they constitute a forest when it is already quite clear that it is a forest.

However, despite these minor faults, Virgo is still endowed with a spirit of friendliness, cordiality and intimacy. In general, people can count on Virgo. Even if they are not an expert in public relations, once they have established a relationship then they usually do not lose or abandon it; part of the reason for this is that when others get to know Virgo well they appreciate their qualities and remain their friends.

When Virgo Gets Angry

Everything that is unexpected or sudden sends Virgo into a tizzy. Virgo detests uncertainty, exaggeration, confusion and disorganization. They don't like to be thrown off balance, wrong-footed or surprised by unforeseen events. For Virgo, everything must consist of rule, order and measure. They must always be in control of a situation. Should a friend deprive them of these sacred linchpins of existence and put them in an uncertain, confused, chaotic condition, their friendship would be damaged.

Virgo is more than punctual, Virgo is hyper-punctual. They arrive at appointments way before the established time. And, they expect others to be equally punctilious and cannot tolerate lateness. In their opinion, arriving late shows an unforgivable lack of respect. They will overlook this the first time it occurs, and forgive it, begrudgingly, the second time; but should someone arrive late for a third time, a firing squad will be waiting. What Virgo absolutely does not tolerate is putting off something that can be done right away. Postponing to an indefinite date is unthinkable for Virgo. A task must be carried out immediately and to the best of one's ability. If they give an order or an assignment, those who are to carry it out must not rest on their laurels or begin and then abandon it, or justify their irresponsible behavior with flimsy excuses. Virgo detests sketchiness, superficiality and laziness. Their inclination – which in many cases becomes almost a fixation – for order and cleanliness is well known. To make Virgo angry one need only get into the Vigo automobile, light a cigarette and let the ash fall on the immaculate seat or mat or go into the perfectly clean and orderly Virgo home with a little dog that sniffs about everywhere or allow children to touch everything and make a mess in every corner. Since Virgo has been well brought up, they probably say nothing in these circumstances. But, one thing is certain and that is that they will never invite that person again.

Virgo
Children

Children born under Virgo are levelheaded, judicious and diligent from very early on, almost like little adults who want to win their parents' affection by being good, obedient and conscientious. They are also very intelligent and learn quickly, and are more comfortable in the company of adults than younger children or those of the same age. In fact, for playmates they prefer older children, from whom they can learn. In general, they like to be with calm children and like to play parlor games that put their intelligence to the test. They do not like roughhouse games or playmates and rarely make friends with irascible and violent youngsters. Virgo children love to read, draw and write, but they are also active and like to be asked to do light manual work because they want to make themselves useful. It is much more likely to see Virgo children active than idle. They are not very curious but, endowed as they are with a sharp mind, they never stop thinking, elaborating, and organizing. They could easily be the top of the class in school, but the innate humility and subtle sense of inadequacy in the Virgo astrological DNA sometimes blocks them. Moreover, their habit of thinking too much is of no help in this regard. Often, they are slow in answering and are 'over-shadowed' by less gifted students, something that makes them suffer. However, they are still among the best in the class, praised by their teachers for their attention and their clear, logical exposition.

Due to their receptive, impressionable soul, which takes in everything that happens in their family life, they should be kept away from arguments that would affect their nervous system. Something else to be avoided are sudden moves and changes, and inexplicable absences, because Virgo children need time to digest and become orientated in a new context or home.

Music Associated

Virgo is a fine organizer, and their well-known finicky character leads them to hear even the tiniest sound that is not right or is out of place, so it is only natural that a leading 20th-century conductor, Leonard Bernstein, should have been born under Virgo. Because, while it is true that music is the magical expression of our deepest feelings, it is also true that one arrives at a concrete result in this field by dint of constant hard practice and study over many years, overcoming the boredom and monotony such application entails. And, technical application certainly does not intimidate or frighten Virgo. Occasionally, their cerebral and overly rational side prevails; an obvious example of this in 20th-century music is the composer Arnold Schönberg. Again, a curious phenomenon in the history of jazz is that all the great, legendary saxophone players are Virgos: Charlie Parker, Lester Young, Sonny Rollins and many others, partly because Virgo corresponds to the fingers (when a planet is located in a bad [weak] position with respect to Virgo, those born under it may suffer from joint pain), so that

with Virgo

one of their leading qualities is having sensitive fingers. All stringed and 'plucked' instruments, in fact, correspond to Virgo, an obvious example being the guitar. Some famous Virgo singers have also written extraordinary poetry, singers such as Leonard Cohen, Roger Waters, Freddie Mercury, Michael Jackson, Liam Gallagher, and Bill Kaulitz. It is indeed strange to see that such a champion of provocation as Amy Winehouse was born under Virgo, but we must bear in mind that, in some cases, reason, order and equilibrium are dangerously transformed into their opposites, when certain planets on one's birth chart suffer bad influences. And, this holds true for such impeccable and great artists as Charlie Parker and Freddie Mercury.

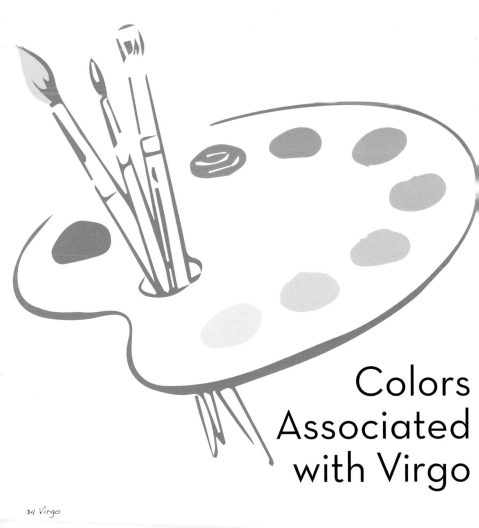

Colors
Associated
with Virgo

Gray – so refined, cold and sophisticated – is the color for Virgo. It is the perfect equilibrium between the white of birth and the black of death; it is an immobile, silent color that lends breadth and luminosity to the other colors. Gray has many different nuances and symbolic meanings; it may refer to old age, but this also implies wisdom, a full life, knowledge and a storehouse of experience. Virgo knows that everything is born and dies and is not afraid of getting old. Virgo is a realist, aware that there is a certain amount of time at their disposal, and they know how to use it to the best of their ability by fortifying their spirit and intelligence, constructing, learning, and finishing what has to be done. The color gray reminds us of gray matter, that is, intelligence, their keen thought processes. But, it may also refer to mediocrity and boredom. However, Virgo is by no means mediocre or banal. They do not like to elbow their way into a crowd or line but prefer to remain in the background. This modesty, the need to shy away from others' judgment, does not mean that they do not count. On the contrary, their qualities leave their mark once they emerge. The field of informatics is also gray: there are 18 hues gray used in computer graphics. Virgo is the sign of technical and technological ability, logical, punctual, and more precise than a computer. Virgo should use slate gray if they want to connect words and thoughts in the best possible way, if they want to listen, understand and above all make themselves understood by others and grasp the essence of others. They should wear platinum gray clothes if they want to lose their self-control, treat themselves to a magical moment of madness, and burn with passion. This is the color that prevails over reluctance, which helps them to lose themselves in the arms of the person they love or in the mists of the unknown. They should choose iron gray when they want to prove their worth. Because at times they are too good and patient, and others take advantage of their spirit of sacrifice.

Flowers
and Plants
Associated
with Virgo

The Virgo constellation is represented as a winged girl holding a shoot and a sheaf of grain, symbols of the continuity of the life cycle. In this period, nature begins a new phase; the earth made arid by the summer heat receives September breezes with joy and prepares for winter. The plants corresponding to Virgo are associated with Mercury, the Virgo ruling planet. These are clover (a Virgo, who is skeptical about nature, would do well to walk in a clover meadow and look for one with four leaves. If they do find one, they should keep it: it will really bring them good luck), hibiscus, orchids, gerberas and the Jerusalem artichoke (*Helianthus Tuberosus*), as well as the yellow daisy which, like a miniature sunflower, reminds us of the summer Sun as we move toward autumn. Ivy is also Virgo because it symbolizes their faithfulness and devotion to the person they love. When they are in love, they are wholly present, and truly at the disposal of and totally clinging to the object of their love, just like ivy.

The flowers and the plants that match the three ten-day periods are as follows.

First period (August 24-September 2): gardenia. This flower with an inebriating fragrance will help stabilize the mind when troubling thoughts arise.

Second period (September 3-12): hyacinth. The name of this flower comes from that of a figure in Greek mythology who was loved by the god Apollo, who accidently killed him. Grow hyacinth in your house in order to have a tender and romantic life as a couple.

Third period (September 13-22): acacia. This is the symbol of Platonic love, immortality and purity. It favors the birth of deep, long-lasting friendship and should be worn if you want a special friend to become a special love.

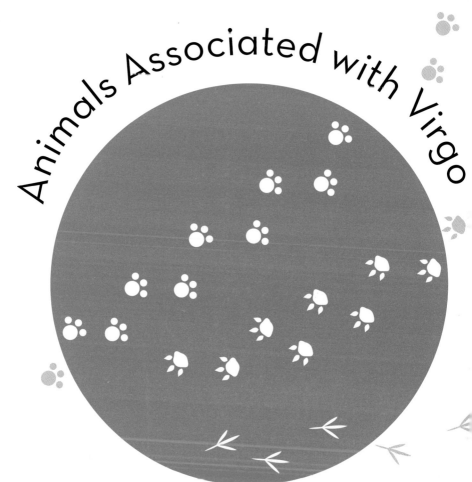

Animals Associated with Virgo

The animal most compatible with Virgo is mythological: the unicorn, a fantastic creature that you might even come upon sooner or later, depicted as a horse with a horn in the middle of its forehead. The unicorn is a symbol of wisdom and purity and, in ancient times, it was believed that it could be approached only by a virgin. It is linked to Virgo because Virgo fascinated by the unusual. Virgo is cerebral and rigorous, and, in real life, wants certainty, not chimeras. It is said that those born under Virgo are, like the Apostle Thomas who doubted the Resurrection: skeptical and mistrustful. But, precisely because Virgo believes only what they actually see, it would do them a world of good to be unsettled, shocked, be immersed in marvelous moments. The unicorn represents their need not to be guided only by reason and self-control. Every so often, they should let themselves be dominated by strong feelings, flashes of madness that awaken the spirit, even if they are mere fantasy, like the unicorn.

The butterfly, on the other hand, symbolizes the lightness of Virgo. Virgo is described as serious and pragmatic, rigid and austere, but this does not always correspond to reality, because they can also be buoyant, merry, light-headed and carefree. They too like a bit of folly and, as light as a butterfly, they alight delicately on the flower of passion. Hard-working creatures are also associated with Virgo, such as the industrious bee, indefatigable mule, ingenious beaver and zealous ant. Among birds, the canary and hummingbird are associated with Virgo. Other corresponding creatures are the quick-footed hare, because Virgo always arrives before others at the heart of the matter, and the turtle, because although Virgo immediately grasps a situation or question, they let themselves be surpassed by those less talented. Lastly, one of the symbolic meanings of Virgo is loyalty, so how could Man's best friend not be associated with Virgo?

Gemstones Associated with Virgo

Among gems and precious crystals, carnelian (also known as cornelian), is particularly compatible with those born under Virgo. The name comes from the Latin *carneus* or flesh colored. This blood-red stone, beloved by the ancient Egyptians, was worn by warriors to give them courage and help them defeat their enemies. Carnelian favors attachment to life and lends one the energy needed to transform an idea into reality. It can be very useful if you are looking for a job, but, above all, it increases the desire for success, makes one more ambitious, helps to focus on aspirations and objectives and gives the strength to realize them. While certain aspects of the Virgo character tend toward modesty, sacrifice and meekness, often leading Virgo to be immobile, carnelian makes Virgo act and react. If worn near the liver and spleen, this gem will help metabolize food.

As for sard, a darker variety of carnelian, it seems that if kept close to the abdomen it will reduce spasms and severe pain. As a Virgo, if you do decide to wear this stone, choose a grayish one. In ancient times, it was used as a protective stone. Besides providing strength and protection in the workplace or home, it will keep away undesirables and will also increase your charm. Again, in ancient times it was thought that this stone could make reluctant persons fall madly in love. If you are courting others who are resisting you, if you want to force the matter and win their heart, you need only give them a sard, which will attract them to you like a magnet.

Another very helpful source of energy for Virgo is smoky quartz, also known as morion and cairngorm. This stone is perfect if you want to increase your stamina, overcome negative feelings, and enhance your strength and determination.

Best Food for Virgo

The correspondence of Virgo with harvests, with the grain stucked up in barns and with cereals, means that pasta, bread, rice and all food containing wheat, oats, corn, barley and rye are compatible with the Virgo diet. Amaranth is perfect due to its positive effect on digestion and its high content of protein, calcium, phosphorus and magnesium. The Romans believed that amaranth warded off envy and mishaps. The Aztecs used it both as food and in their religious ceremonies, and called it 'the wheat of the gods', while for the Incas it was *Kiwicha* or 'the little giant'. In the past, people believed that those who kept the amaranth flower with them at all times would preserve their health and youth. Quinoa is also a sacred plant and food that is connected to Virgo. The Incas called it *Chisiya Mama*, 'the mother of all seeds'. It has excellent nutritional properties, high protein content and no gluten at all. Besides being a food, cereals can also be used as small good luck charms by mixing the seeds in a bowl and keeping them by your side, whether in the workplace or at home, much like good genies who watch over one's well-being.

Other, typically Virgo, foods are fennel, celery and all soft fruit: whortleberries, gooseberries, blackberries, currants and raspberries, as well as cherries, cherry plums and strawberries. Among the aromatic plants, Virgo prefers sage and oregano. In the Middle Ages, girls who wanted to find their true love and get married placed a twig of sage under their pillows. Besides propitiating a meeting with the right person and seasoning food, sage, the typical health herb, has many pharmacological properties. For Virgo, Oregano, which is used quite a lot in the typical Mediterranean diet, also has fine therapeutic proprieties and wards off sadness.

Myths
Associated
with Virgo

Ceres, the Roman goddess and protector of vegetation, cereals and agriculture, is closely connected to Virgo. The goddess was depicted with her head adorned with sheaves and flowers and holding a sheaf or a basket full of grain and fruit in her hand. Three feasts were dedicated to her - August 10, October 10 and eight days in April, from the 12th to the 19th - all days in which Virgo too can connect with the generating power symbolized by the goddess. Ceres represents the relationship Virgo has with the earth, and their solidity, manual dexterity, their fertile and creative side - as well as altruism and the care and devotion with which they do everything. Just as Ceres gave fruit, flowers and life to humans, Virgo gives everything of themselves and constantly care for those they love. This maternal goddess symbolizes their capacity for thoughtfulness. As regards love, Virgo is constructive and, with their partner, are faithful and devoted, not only in the form of tender feelings, but also, and above all, as concrete facts and real support. The Virgo sign corresponds to gardening and botany, and Virgo often has green fingers and love to be in touch with plants and flowers.

There is a Virgo connected to Ceres as well as a Virgo closely linked with Mercury, the god of intelligence, reason, eloquence and commerce. This latter, mercurial Virgo is nervous, always oscillating between bad and good moods, between satisfaction and dissatisfaction, serenity and agitation. The undisputed qualities of intelligence and an analytical mind, in Virgo, can become a handicap if continuous mental activity should prevail over the voice of their heart. The analogy with Mercury makes them the sign of logic, while the correspondence with Ceres means that they are the sign of vitality. The ideal would be to merge their rational and creative sides, their mind and their heart.

Virgo Fairy Tale

Cinderella is a famous fairy tale, known in most of the world in various versions. In Perrault's version, she is a beautiful young girl whose mother has died and whose father remarries an evil woman who has two equally evil daughters. Unfortunately, her father also dies, so Cinderella is left alone with a wicked stepmother who makes her work as a servant, forced to clean, serve and obey. As is the case with many fables, a handsome prince saves the day. With the help of a fairy, Cinderella is able to go to the prince's ball, where he falls in love with her. But, at midnight, she has to return home and, in her haste, loses a slipper. However, the prince, thanks to the slipper, finds and marries Cinderella, who thus becomes a princess, much to the dismay of her humiliated stepmother and stepsisters. In this fairy tale, we have the industriousness, the humility, and the power of resistance that are distinguishing features of those born under Virgo. Virgo is the sign of material and mental order, of attention paid to things, of methodical and humble behavior and activity, with a sense of sacrifice that is quite often rewarded. Like Cinderella, Virgo tends to have a gentle character and is patient. If they must, they can adapt to a humble life, but they do so happily only if they feel they are useful, if they are devoting their efforts to something important, for those they love or for an ideal. Their tendency to suddenly break off a relationship if they think they have been treated unjustly is represented by Cinderella hastily leaving the ball at midnight.

Cinderella's dreary life is also a warning: too much reasoning, abnegation, humility and frugality, and too much arid thought, suffocate the joys of life and lead to a bleak existence. For Virgo, if dissatisfaction makes their daily life dull and bleak, they will not be able to wait for the prince to arrive. No, they must act decisively, take their life in their hands and set it in the direction they want it to take.

PATRIZIA TRONI, trained at the school of Marco Pesatori, writes the astrology columns for Italian magazines *Marie Claire* and *Telepiù*. She has worked in the most important astrology magazines (*Astra, Sirio, Astrella, Minima Astrologica*), she has edited and written the astrology supplement of *TV Sorrisi e Canzoni* and *Chi* for years, and she is an expert not only in contemporary astrology, but also in Arab and Renaissance astrology.

Photo Credits
Archivio White Star pages 28, 34, 38; artizarus/123RF page 20 center; Cihan Demirok/123RF pages 1, 2, 3, 4, 14, 30, 48; Yvette Fain/123RF page 46; file404/123RF page 16 bottom; Olexandr Kovernik/123RF page 42; Valerii Matviienko/123RF pages 8, 12; murphy81/Shutterstock page 44; Igor Nazarenko/123RF page 40; Michalis Panagiotidis/123RF pages 20, 21; tribalium123/123RF page 16; Maria Zaynullina/123RF page 36

WHITE STAR PUBLISHERS

WS White Star Publishers® is a registered trademark property of De Agostini Libri S.p.A.

© 2015 De Agostini Libri S.p.A.
Via G. da Verrazano, 15 - 28100 Novara, Italy
www.whitestar.it - www.deagostini.it

Translation: Richard Pierce - Editing: Norman Gilligan

All rights reserved. No part of this publication may be reproduced, stored in a retrieval system or transmitted in any form or by any means, electronic, mechanical, photocopying, recording or otherwise, without written permission from the publisher.

ISBN 978-88-544-0968-2
1 2 3 4 5 6   19 18 17 16 15
Printed in China